REBEL GiRLS

STICK TOGETHER

A Sticker-by-Number Book

DIAL BOOKS FOR YOUNG READERS

Dial Books for Young Readers
An imprint of Penguin Random House LLC, New York

First published in the United States of America by Dial Books for Young Readers,
an imprint of Penguin Random House LLC, 2021

Dial & colophon are registered trademarks of Penguin Random House LLC.
Visit us online at penguinrandomhouse.com.
Good Night Stories for Rebel Girls and Rebel Girls are trademarks of Rebel Girls, Inc.

Manufactured in China
ISBN 9780593407233

10 9 8 7 6 5 4 3 2 1

Design by Jennifer Kelly
Text set in Montserrat and Woolwich

HELLO, REBEL GIRL!

We hope that these twelve extraordinary heroes will fascinate and inspire you. We've included activists, artists, and athletes from all around the world who range in time from 69 B.C. to the present. These girls and women are pioneers who have let their convictions and curiosity guide them.

May you follow their lead in your own life.

MAY YOU DREAM BIGGER, AIM HIGHER, AND FIGHT HARDER!

HOW TO USE THIS BOOK

There is a page of stickers at the end of the book for each of the twelve puzzles included. Match the numbered sticker to the numbered space in the puzzle. Each portrait is perforated, so when you've finished a picture, you can carefully tear it out of the book to hang on your wall. Each sticker page is also perforated, so you can tear out those pages for easier stickering.

The finished pictures are all previewed on the first few pages, along with a bit of information about each of the heroic women.

Amelia Earhart
Aviator
July 24, 1897–circa July 1937
United States of America

Amelia Earhart was the first woman to fly solo across the Atlantic Ocean. She loved to do things no one had ever done before. "Adventure is worthwhile in itself," she said. And in fact, she was in the middle of her greatest adventure, trying to fly all the way around the world, when her plane disappeared somewhere over the Pacific Ocean. She was never found, but her bravery and accomplishments will never be forgotten.

Illustration by Giulia Flamini

Beatrice Vio
Fencer
Born March 4, 1997
Italy

From the age of five, Beatrice Vio, better known as Bebe, loved the sport of fencing. When she was eleven, she contracted meningitis, an illness so severe that the doctors had to amputate her legs and forearms to save her. But Bebe didn't give up her dream of fencing competitively. She relearned to walk and then started training again. Less than ten years later, she had won multiple championships and a gold medal at the Paralympic Games.

Illustration by Cristina Portolano

Beyoncé
Singer, Songwriter
Born September 4, 1981
United States of America

Beyoncé, the most-nominated woman in the history of the Grammy Awards, was already performing as a singer and dancer at the age of six. As a child, she joined a band that later became the chart-topping Destiny's Child. Eventually she became one of the most influential pop stars in the world, singing about freedom, love, and social justice. She has inspired millions of women to be proud of their culture and uniqueness.

Illustration by Eline Van Dam

Celia Cruz
Singer
October 21, 1925–July 16, 2003
Cuba

Celia Cruz, born in Havana, Cuba, was always singing. Although her father wanted her to become a teacher, she couldn't abandon her love of music. She jumped at the chance to sing in the popular band Sonora Matancera. When revolution broke out in Cuba, Celia and her band found their way to the United States, where her big personality and amazing voice helped to make salsa music wildly popular. She was the undisputed Queen of Salsa for forty years.

Illustration by Ping Zhu

Cleopatra
Pharaoh
69 B.C.–August 12, 30 B.C.
Egypt

Cleopatra wouldn't let her brother steal the kingdom from her. When Julius Caesar, the emperor of ancient Rome, came to Egypt to help resolve their battle, Cleopatra made sure to get time with Caesar by smuggling herself into his rooms rolled inside a carpet. He was so impressed by her daring that he restored her to the throne. When she died years later, the empire ended with her. Cleopatra was the last pharaoh to rule Egypt.

Illustration by Kiki Ljung

Frida Kahlo
Painter
July 6, 1907–July 13, 1954
Mexico

When Frida Kahlo was six, she nearly died from polio. The disease left her with a permanent limp, but it didn't destroy her lively spirit. And then, when she was eighteen, she was involved in a bus accident and nearly died again. During the months she spent recovering in bed, she began painting portraits of herself—and unlocked an enormous talent that would make her one of the most famous artists in the world.

Illustration by Helena Morais Soares

Jane Goodall
Primatologist
Born April 3, 1934
United Kingdom

Young Jane Goodall loved climbing trees and reading books, and most of all, she loved animals. That passion led her as an adult to Tanzania, where she studied chimpanzees in their natural environment for many, many years. With patience, scientific observation, and tenderness, Jane discovered amazing things about chimpanzees, including the surprising facts that they are not vegetarians and that they make and use tools.

Illustration by Emanuelle Walker

Malala Yousafzai
Activist
Born July 12, 1997
Pakistan

Malala Yousafzai grew up in Pakistan. When the Taliban, a militant group, took control of her country and forbade girls from attending school, Malala dared to speak out. "The Taliban don't want women to be powerful," she said on TV. A few days later, two Taliban men shot her in retaliation. But Malala lived, continued to fight for the rights of girls and women, and became the youngest person ever to receive the Nobel Peace Prize.

Illustration by Sara Bondi

Rosa Parks
Activist
February 4, 1913–October 24, 2005
United States of America

Montgomery, Alabama, was a segregated city for much of Rosa Parks's life. Black people were not allowed to attend the same schools, drink from the same water fountains, or sit in the same bus seats as white people. One day Rosa was asked to give up her seat on a bus so a white person could sit. When she said no, her courage inspired a boycott that lasted more than a year and ended with the U.S. Supreme Court declaring bus segregation unconstitutional.

Illustration by Sally Nixon

Ruth Bader Ginsburg
Supreme Court Justice
March 15, 1933–September 18, 2020
United States of America

When Ruth Bader Ginsburg was a girl, most lawyers and judges were men. But Ruth dreamed of being a great lawyer, and she accomplished that goal and much more. She successfully argued six landmark cases on gender equality before the U.S. Supreme Court. Then she became a Supreme Court Justice—only the second female justice in the country's history. Her dissenting opinions during the twenty-seven years she served on the country's highest court helped to shape minds and laws.

Illustration by Eleanor Davis

Simone Biles
Gymnast

Born March 14, 1997
United States of America

Simone Biles, who started gymnastics when she was six years old, has won more World Gymnastics Championship medals than any other athlete. At the 2016 Olympic Games, she won five medals—four of them gold! Many say she is the best gymnast who has ever lived. But she says that "a medal can't be a goal." When she gets on the mat, her goal is simply to do her best.

Illustration by Eline Van Dam

Yusra Mardini
Swimmer

Born March 5, 1998
Syria

Swimmer Yusra Mardini and her sister fled their war-torn country of Syria after a bomb destroyed their home. They were on a boat with other refugees, trying to make their way to Greece, when the boat's motor broke down. Yusra and a few other swimmers jumped into the ocean and kept that dinghy afloat for more than three hours, saving the lives of all twenty refugees. A year later, Yusra swam in the Olympics as part of the first refugee team to ever take part in that competition.

Illustration by Jessica Cooper

AMELIA EARHART

BEATRICE VIO

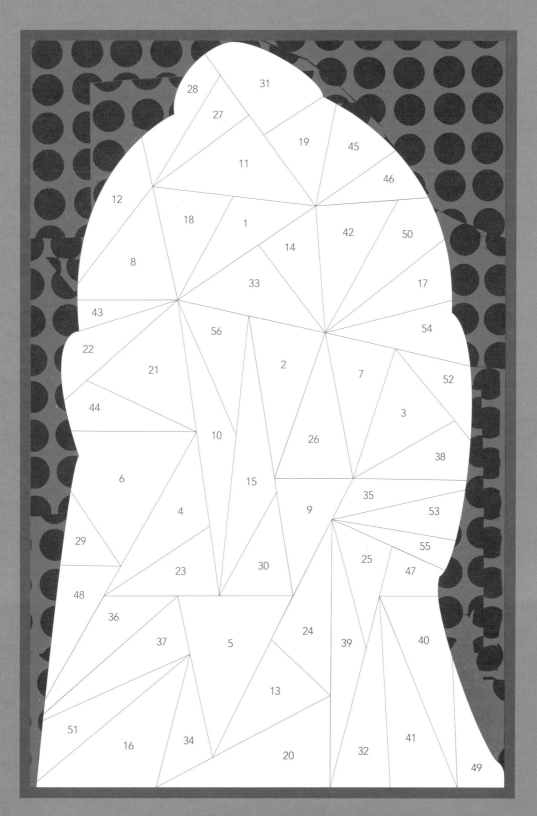

BEYONCÉ

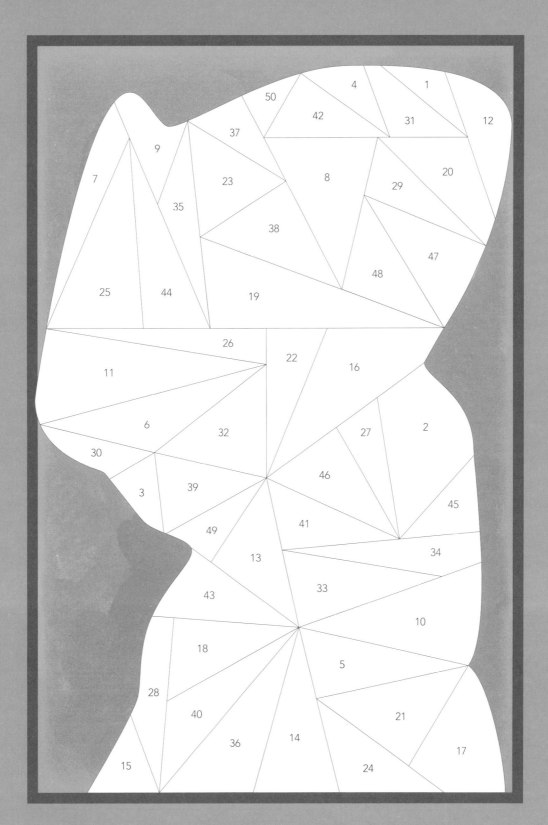

CELIA CRUZ

CLEOPATRA

FRIDA KAHLO

JANE GOODALL

MALALA YOUSAFZAI

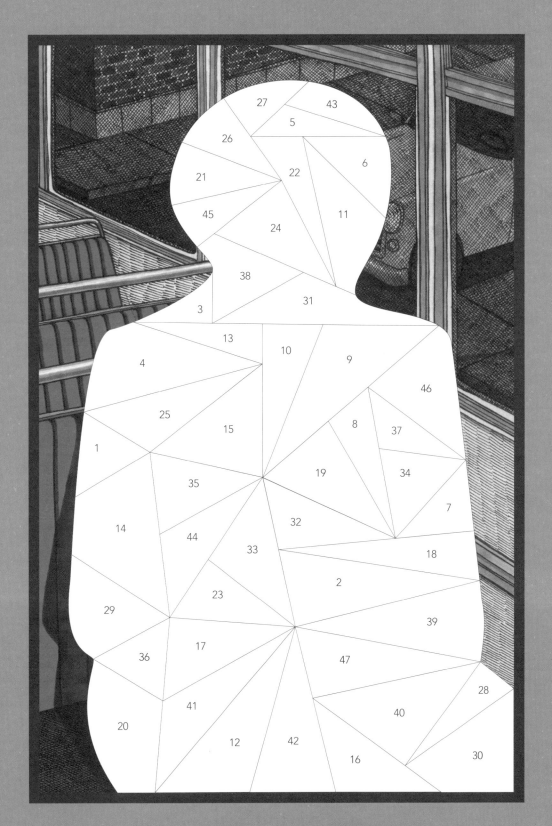

ROSA PARKS

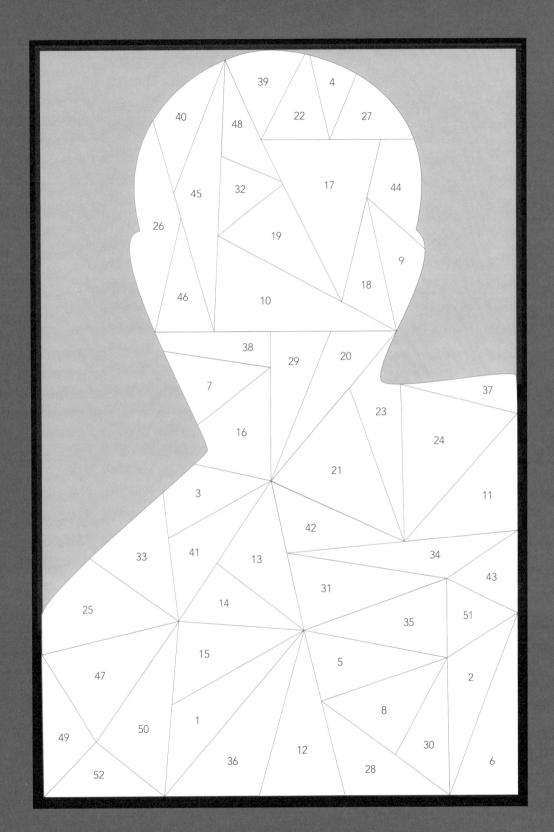

RUTH BADER GINSBURG

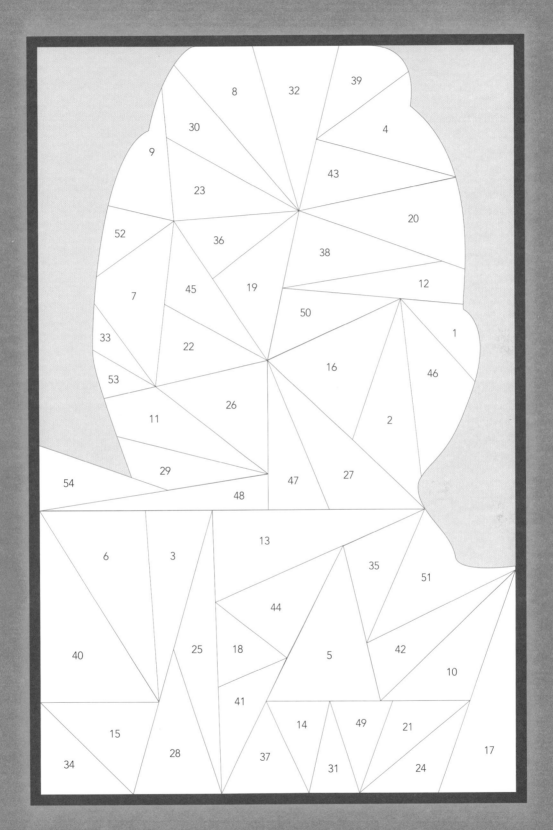

SIMONE BILES

YUSRA MARDINI